# American Football

## THIS EDITION
**Produced for DK** by WonderLab Group LLC
Jennifer Emmett, Erica Green, Kate Hale, *Founders*

**Editor** Maya Myers; **Photography Editor** Nicole DiMella; **Managing Editor** Rachel Houghton;
**Designers** Project Design Company; **Researcher** Michelle Harris; **Copy Editor** Lori Merritt;
**Indexer** Connie Binder; **Proofreader** Susan K. Hom; **Series Reading Specialist** Dr Jennifer Albro

This edition published in 2025
First published in Great Britain in 2025 by
Dorling Kindersley Limited
20 Vauxhall Bridge Road,
London SW1V 2SA

The authorised representative in the EEA is
Dorling Kindersley Verlag GmbH. Arnulfstr. 124,
80636 Munich, Germany

Copyright © 2025 Dorling Kindersley Limited
24 25 26 27 10 9 8 7 6 5 4 3 2 1
001–345669–June/2025

All rights reserved.
Without limiting the rights under the copyright reserved above, no part of this publication may be reproduced, stored in or introduced into a retrieval system, or transmitted, in any form, or by any means (electronic, mechanical, photocopying, recording, or otherwise), without the prior written permission of the copyright owner.
Published in Great Britain by Dorling Kindersley Limited

A CIP catalogue record for this book
is available from the British Library.
ISBN: 978-0-2417-2384-5

Printed and bound in China

Super Readers Lexile® levels 620L to 790L
Lexile® is the registered trademark of MetaMetrics, Inc. Copyright © 2024 MetaMetrics, Inc. All rights reserved.

The publisher would like to thank the following for their kind permission to reproduce their images:
a=above; c=centre; b=below; l=left; r=right; t=top; b/g=background

**123RF.com:** aomarch 8t; **Alamy Stock Photo:** John Jones / Icon Sportswire / AP Images 16, Chicago Tribune file photo / TNS / McClatchy-Tribune 44cl, Bill Craft 11b, Burt Granofsky / CSM 13t, Darren Lee / CSM 33t, Duncan Williams / CSM 21t, 41br, Jevone Moore / CSM 15b, Mario Houben / CSM 9br, Mike Buscher / CSM 26br, Bob Daemmrich 7br, Kirby Lee 20, 32, Ross Pelton / MediaPunch 19tr, PCN Photography 36, Rich Kane Photography 19cl, Nhat V. Meyer / Bay Area News Group / TNS / Sipa USA 26tl, Tribune Content Agency LLC / Kenneth K. Lam / Baltimore Sun / McClatchy-Tribune 42, John Angelillo / UPI 1, 6-7, 33b, Jon SooHoo / UPI 22, Kevin Dietsch / UPI 15t, Kevin M. Cox / UPI 6br, UPI Photo / Bill Greenblatt 45tr, Al Golub / ZUMA Press Wire 21b, Brent Gudenschwager / ZUMA Press Wire 35cra, Ringo Chiu / ZUMA Press Wire 26-27, Scott Coleman / ZUMA Wire 8b, Scott Stuart / ZUMA Press Wire 3, Zuma Press, Inc. / Jose Luis Villegas12 / 17 / 00 Sacramento B 31br, David Roseblum / Southcreek Global / ZUMApress.com 19br; **Depositphotos Inc:** jbcalom 39bl; **Dreamstime.com:** Enterlinedesign 28b, Aleksei Gorodenkov 4-5; **Getty Images:** AFP / Paul Buck / Stringer 41tr, Bruce Bennett 11tl, 30, Bettmann 17cl, 17br, 23, 40, Wally Mcnamee / Corbis 18cr, Diamond Images / Kidwiler Collection 45tl, David Eulitt / Stringer 14, Nate Fine 17tr, James Flores 12, Focus On Sport 13b, 18t, 24-25, 25bl, 31tr, 37cl, 39tl, Ralph Freso / Stringer 9, George Gelatly 11tr, George Gojkovich 39cr, Hulton Archive / Allsport / Damian Strohmeyer 25tr, Ryan Kang 37br, MediaNews Group / Boston Herald / Matt Stone 31cl, Ethan Miller / Staff 34-35t, Christian Petersen / Staff 45bl, Todd Rosenberg 41cl, Gregory Shamus / Staff 20bl, Sporting News Archive 43, Carlos Gonzalez / Star Tribune 28-29, Tony Tomsic 37tr, 38, 44br; **Getty Images / iStock:** E+ / Dmytro Aksonov 44-45; **Library of Congress, Washington, D.C.:** LC-DIG-ggbain-09741 / Bain News Service, publisher 10tr, LC-DIG-hec-29359 / Harris & Ewing 10cl, LC-USZ62-33728 / Corner Bookstore (Ithaca, N.Y.) 10br

Cover images: *Front:* **Alamy Stock Photo:** Duncan Williams / Cal Sport Media / Sipa USA bc, Jevone Moore / CSM / Sipa USA r, Ian Halperin / UPI br; **Getty Images:** Chris Unger / Stringer l; **Getty Images / iStock:** E+ / Dmytro Aksonov;
*Back:* **Dreamstime.com:** Lio Putra cla; **Getty Images / iStock:** Fendy Hermawan cra; **Shutterstock.com:** pikepicture cl

www.dk.com

This book was made with Forest Stewardship Council™ certified paper – one small step in DK's commitment to a sustainable future.
Learn more at www.dk.com/uk/information/sustainability

Level 3

# American Football

James Buckley Jr.

# Contents

**6**  Kickoff!
**10** NFL History
**14** Prime Passers
**22** Rushing Runners
**28** Remarkable Receivers

**34** Dominant Defenders
**42** Clutch Kickers
**44** Championship Coaches
**46** Glossary
**47** Index
**48** Quiz

# Kickoff!

American football is the US's most popular sport. Tens of millions of people watch games on TV. Millions more attend school, college and professional games in person. The annual championship game for the National Football League (NFL) is called the Super Bowl. In 2024, the game attracted 123 million viewers. That's the most people to watch a sports event ... ever!

What are all those fans watching? They're cheering for hard-hitting, fast-moving, dramatic action. Players smack into each other with great force. They wear lots of gear to help keep them safe.

College teams like University of Michigan have millions of fans.

Super Bowl action

### Friday Night Lights
In many parts of the US, school American football is more than a sport. It's a tradition. On Friday nights, the community gathers to cheer on the local school team. Some of those players go on to play for college teams. College teams compete to become the national college champion each year.

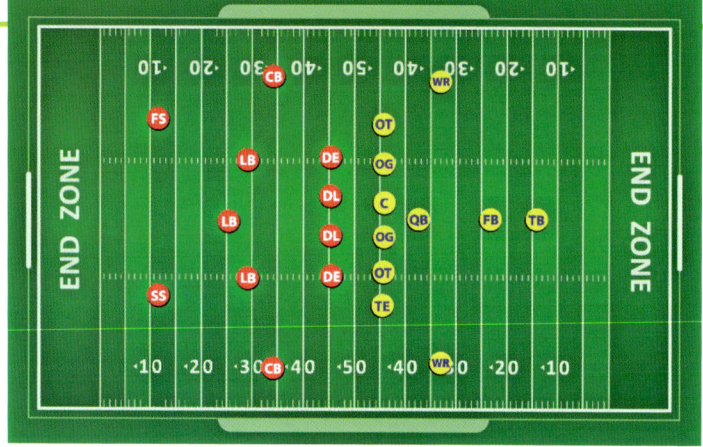

In American football, two teams of 11 players face off on a field. The field is 100 yards long. At both ends are spaces called end zones. The team that has the football tries to move towards the opposite end zone. That's where they can score a touchdown (TD) for six points. As they move, the other team tries to stop them.

To move, teams can carry the ball until the ballcarrier is knocked down, or tackled. They can pass the ball, too. After a catch, the receiver can run until he gets tackled.

The seven officials on the field enforce rules and call penalties when rules are broken.

The team that has the ball is called the offence. It gets four tries, or downs, to move at least 10 yards down the field. The other team is called the defence. It tries to prevent runs and passes. When a player is tackled, that play is over. There are lots of rules to follow. The teams use different strategies to win.

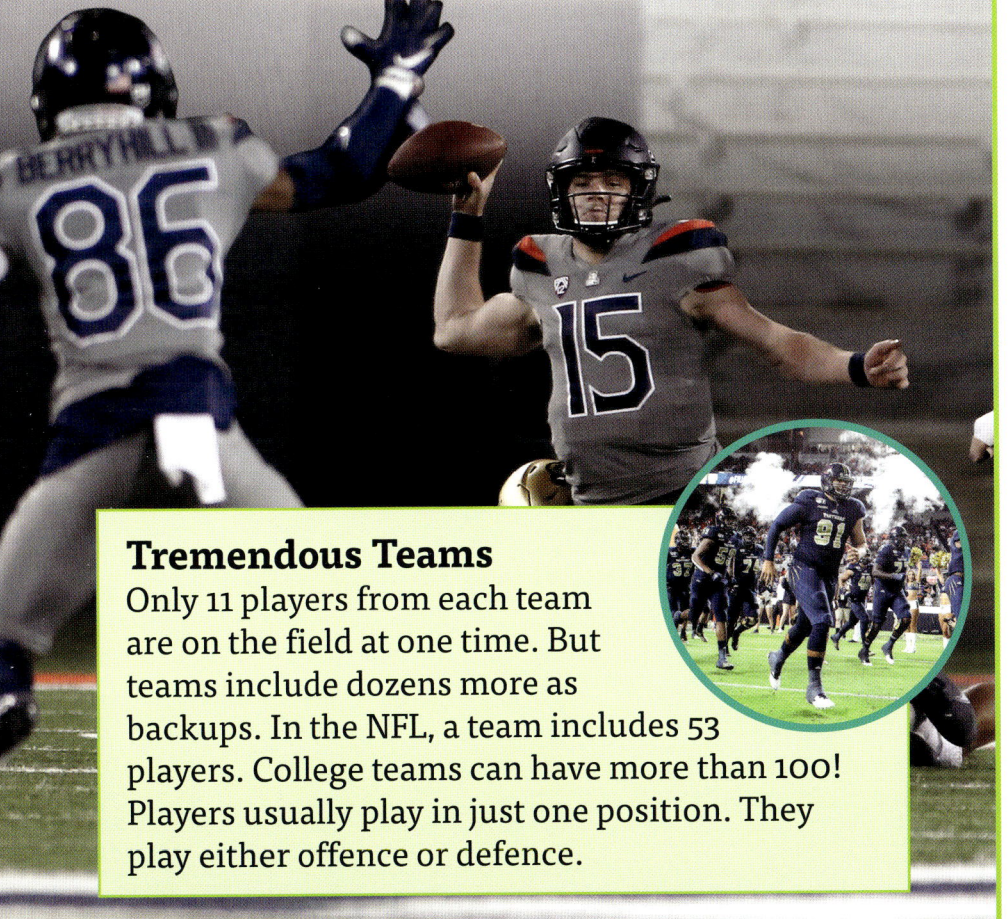

### Tremendous Teams
Only 11 players from each team are on the field at one time. But teams include dozens more as backups. In the NFL, a team includes 53 players. College teams can have more than 100! Players usually play in just one position. They play either offence or defence.

# NFL History

For centuries, people have been kicking balls around for fun. In the middle of the 1800s, two ball-kicking games became popular in England. One was the game Americans now call soccer. The other was rugby.

In the US at about the same time, a form of American football became popular at colleges on the East Coast. The early form of the game was all running, no passing. No one wore safety pads. It was incredibly dangerous.

Above: Around 1915; right: Cornell University team, 1913

Left: Norman Barr, University of Pennsylvania, 1910s; right: Otto Graham in an NFL championship game, 1952; below: the first pro-league champions, the Akron Professionals

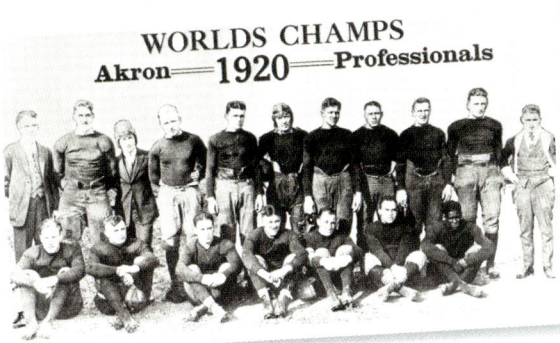

In 1905, President Teddy Roosevelt stepped in. He enforced new rules that helped reduce violence. American football got safer. Soon, college football was one of America's biggest sports.

A pro league was started in Ohio in 1920. In 1922, its name changed to the NFL. It had 14 teams, mostly from the Midwest. By the 1950s, NFL games were shown on TV.

Super Bowl I, 1967

The first Super Bowl was in 1967. By that time, many homes in the US had a TV. Now almost everyone could watch games from home and the NFL skyrocketed in popularity. Regular-season games sold out all over the country. The NFL was worth many billions of dollars. Players were paid more, too.

## Women's Football Alliance

Since 2009, the Women's Football Alliance (WFA) has held annual seasons for women to strap on helmets and play. Women have played American football at school and college. Some have worked as coaches in the NFL.

Allison Cahill

Players from 100 years ago could not imagine how big the NFL has become today. Let's meet some of the NFL's greatest players from the past and the present.

Emmitt Smith

# Prime Passers

*Fans in Arrowhead Stadium are screaming. Patrick Mahomes drops back to pass. The Kansas City Chiefs quarterback (QB) scrambles, looking for a receiver. He spots one downfield. He throws a perfect spiral. The ball zips past defenders and into the arms of teammate Travis Kelce. Kelce knocks over a tackler. He dives into the end zone.* **Touchdown!**

Patrick Mahomes

## Tom Brady
### The GOAT

Before he retired in 2023, Tom Brady led his teams to seven Super Bowl wins. This is far more than any other QB. He won six with the New England Patriots and one with the Tampa Bay Buccaneers.

The QB is the most important player on a team. QBs have to be able to throw perfect passes. They also have to run fast and avoid tacklers. They are leaders who inspire their teams. Mahomes has great passing and leadership abilities. He once threw 50 TD passes in one season. That's the second-most of all time! He has also led his team to three Super Bowl championships.

When American football started, passing the ball was against the rules! It became a common part of the game by the 1910s. Teams could gain more yards quickly by passing.

Three players in the first decades of the NFL helped make the role of the QB what it is today.

Jalen Hurts

"Slingin'" **Sammy Baugh** was a tremendous athlete. Along with being a top passer for the Washington, DC NFL team, he was a great punter. He played offence and defence!

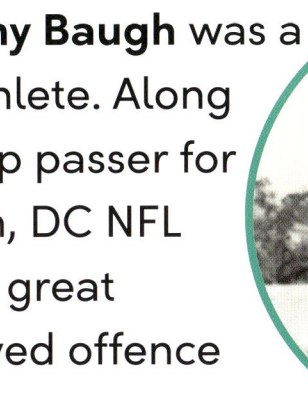

**Sid Luckman** was the QB for the Chicago Bears for 12 years. He led them to four NFL championships. Luckman was big and strong. He helped turn the QB into the game's key position.

**Otto Graham** was an exceptional leader. He was a star basketball player before he played American football. He guided the Cleveland Browns to a record 10 championship games starting in 1946. His teams won seven of them!

From the 1960s onwards, passing became the most important part of the game. For many years, **Johnny Unitas** was considered the best QB of all time. From 1956 to 1973, Unitas set new records for touchdown passes with the Baltimore Colts. He was also the first to lead a two-minute drill: a rapid series of plays as time ran out in the game.

In the 1980s, **Joe Montana** took over the title of best QB ever. He led the San Francisco 49ers to four Super Bowl titles.

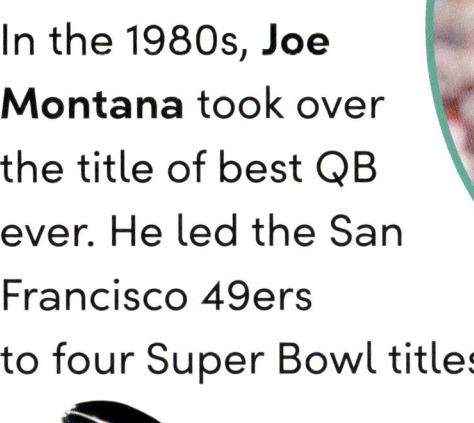

**John Elway** broke many NFL records. He guided the Denver Broncos to a pair of championships in the 1990s.

In the early 21st century, **Peyton Manning** led both the Indianapolis Colts and the Broncos to Super Bowl wins. Before Brady, Manning held most of the NFL's career passing records.

Patrick Mahomes has some competition for today's top NFL QB. **Lamar Jackson** of the Baltimore Ravens is a two-time NFL most valuable player (MVP). Along with passing, Jackson's top skill is running. He has set several QB records for running with the ball.

### Choosing Players
Each April, NFL teams choose new players at the NFL Draft. They select college players to join their teams. Teams with the lowest records from the previous season get to choose first in the draft.

Like Jackson, **Josh Allen** of the Buffalo Bills is a great runner and passer. Allen has scored 53 rushing TDs, second-most ever among QBs.

**Brock Purdy** leads the San Francisco 49ers. Purdy was the last player chosen in the 2022 NFL Draft. But he became the starter and led the team to the Super Bowl in 2023 – where he lost to Mahomes and the Chiefs!

Christian McCaffrey being tackled by Jalen Ramsey

## Rushing Runners

*The ball is snapped and QB Brock Purdy hands the ball to running back Christian McCaffrey. McCaffrey sprints forward. He looks for a hole in the line of defensive players. His blockers create a tiny space between defenders. McCaffrey races through it! He dodges a tackler, shoves another away and he's off! Next stop: the end zone and six points.*

## Pioneers

Until 1946, the NFL had nearly all white players, mostly because of the racism of team owners. But that year, four Black players joined the league: Marion Motley, Woody Strode, Kenny Washington and Bill Willis. Running back Motley became one of the best players in league history. With the door opened, thousands of Black players were able to play. By 2024, more than half of the NFL players were Black.

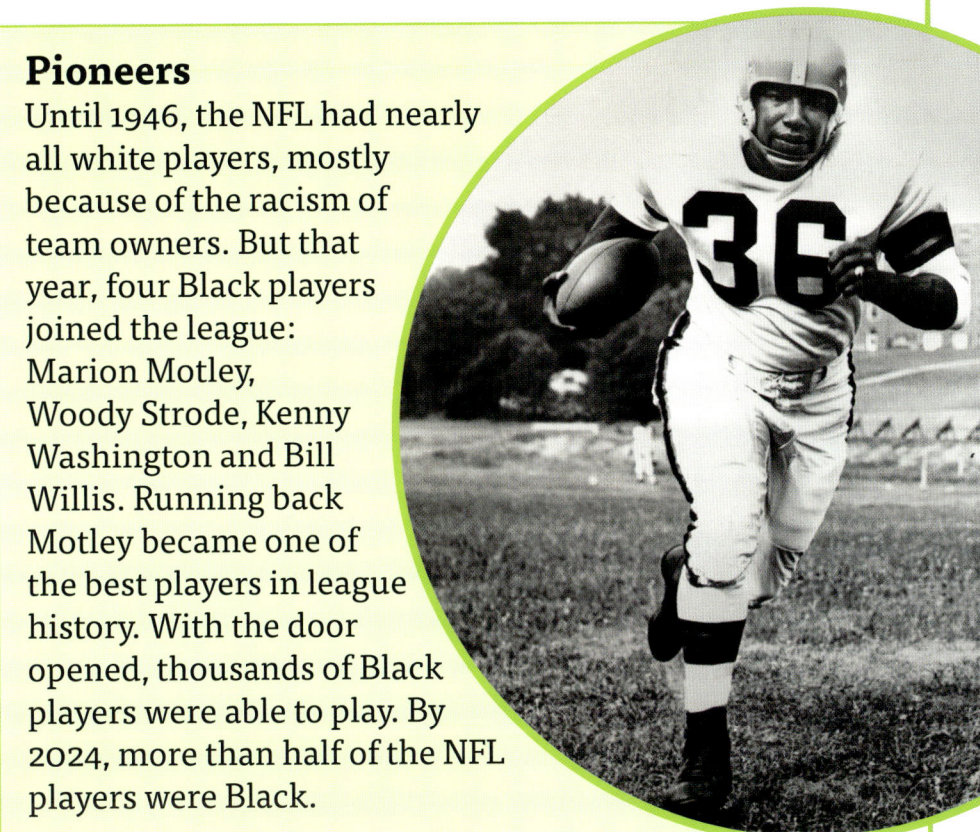

Marion Motley

Most teams use runs for about half of their plays. The key person for running is the running back (RB, or halfback). Running backs are fast, strong and durable. The distance they run with the ball is called rushing yards. The best running backs hope to rush the ball for 1,000 yards or more each season.

Running back **Walter Payton** of the Chicago Bears was nicknamed "Sweetness" for his personality. But on the field, he was not very sweet to defenders. When he retired in 1987, he was the NFL's all-time leader in rushing yards. He had hip-swivelling moves and could leap over defenders.

The best running backs can dodge tacklers and knock over defenders. **Barry Sanders** ran like he was on roller skates. His quick cuts and sharp turns left tacklers grabbing air. Sanders ran for more than 1,300 yards in nine of his 10 seasons with the Detroit Lions. For four of those seasons, he led the NFL in rushing.

### Jim Brown
#### The RB GOAT

Our vote for the NFL running back GOAT is Jim Brown. He led the NFL in rushing eight times in the 1950s and 1960s. Brown combined power with great speed. It often took several defenders to tackle him.

**Christian McCaffrey** is among the best runners in the NFL. He is very fast and strong enough to break tackles. In 2019, he set an NFL record with 2,392 yards rushing and receiving combined. In 2023, playing for the San Francisco 49ers, he led the NFL in rushing yards.

Powerful **Derrick Henry** joined the Baltimore Ravens in 2024. Before that, he played for the Tennessee Titans. With the Titans, Henry had three seasons with over 1,500 rushing yards. Henry is almost impossible to tackle once he gets rolling.

Other top RBs in the NFL today are **Kyren Williams** of the Los Angeles Rams, D'Andre Swift of the Chicago Bears and James Cook of the Buffalo Bills.

# Remarkable Receivers

*Justin Jefferson sprints down the field, then zigzags to avoid a defender. Running at full speed, he looks up, sees the football flying through the air ... and leaps! Jefferson grabs the ball, then lands with a thud in the end zone. Another TD catch!*

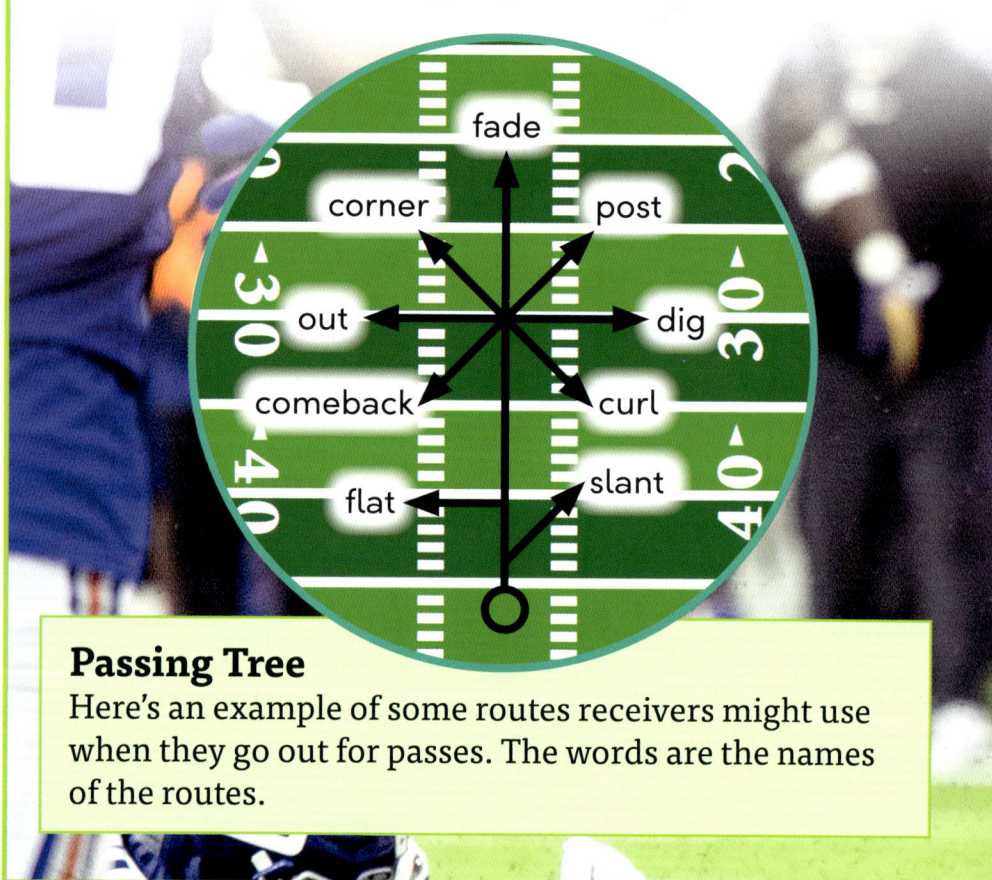

**Passing Tree**
Here's an example of some routes receivers might use when they go out for passes. The words are the names of the routes.

Jefferson is one of many dynamic receivers. Receivers catch the ball. They need speed, great moves and jumping ability. The QB assigns a route on each play. Routes are the paths the receivers will run. The QB often throws the pass while the receiver is still running. So, it is very important for the receiver to go exactly where the QB tells him to go.

Justin Jefferson scoring a touchdown

In American football's early days, receivers played a smaller role. Green Bay's **Don Hutson** changed that. In 1942, he caught 74 passes – almost three times as many as anyone else that year! Hutson led the NFL in catches eight times and caught 99 TD passes. At the time, this was the most ever.

By the 1980s, **Steve Largent** of the Seattle Seahawks had broken many of Hutson's NFL records.

Wide receiver (WR) **Randy Moss** led the NFL in TD catches five times, including a record 23 in 2007.

### Jerry Rice
**The WR GOAT**

Rice holds just about every important NFL record for pass-catchers. He played most of his career with the San Francisco 49ers. In his 20 seasons, he scored more touchdowns (208) than any player ever!

The NFL is filled with great receivers. Dozens of tall, speedy, glue-fingered players score points every weekend.

Minnesota's **Justin Jefferson** is among the most exciting. He catches just about everything thrown his way. He even makes catches when defences double-team him. That means two defenders track him on the field at the same time.

**CeeDee Lamb** broke several Dallas Cowboys records in 2023. He made 135 catches, the most of anyone in the NFL.

**Tyreek Hill** showed off his speed while helping the Chiefs win the Super Bowl in 2019. He moved to Miami in 2022. He had more than 1,700 yards receiving in each of his first two seasons with the Dolphins.

T. J. Watt (left) trying to sack Jimmy Garoppolo

## Dominant Defenders

*T. J. Watt races forward as the ball is snapped. The Pittsburgh Steelers linebacker smacks into a blocker, then shoves him aside. Watt spins past another player, then crashes into the quarterback, knocking him down. It's a sack!*

Stopping the NFL's great players on offence takes speed, toughness, intelligence and courage. There are three types of defenders.

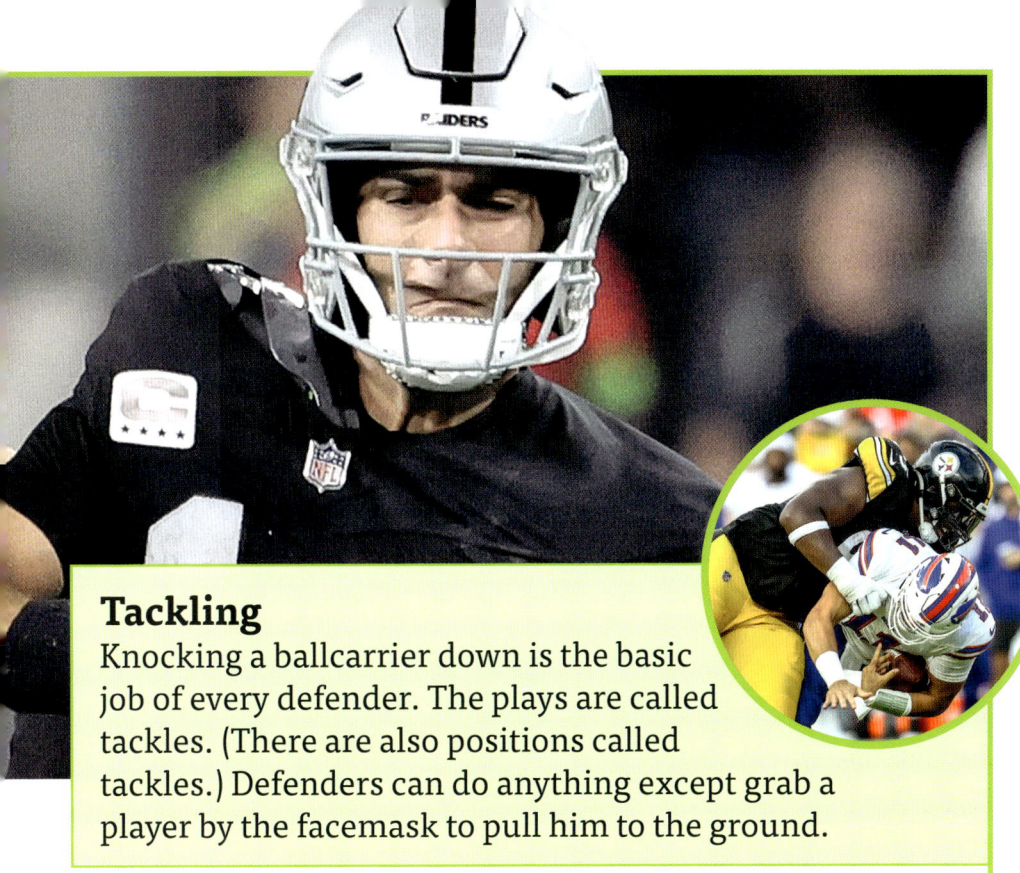

### Tackling
Knocking a ballcarrier down is the basic job of every defender. The plays are called tackles. (There are also positions called tackles.) Defenders can do anything except grab a player by the facemask to pull him to the ground.

Defensive linemen start closest to the ball. They focus on stopping runners. They also rush the quarterback for sacks.

Linebackers come next. They need to be fast and strong to chase running backs and quarterbacks. They also try to stop receivers.

Defensive backs are the fastest players on the field. They chase down receivers and try to keep them from catching passes.

A quarterback sack is one of a defence's favourite moments. It pushes the offence back. It also makes the passer a bit nervous for the next play! Players who are sack masters become big stars.

### Lawrence Taylor
**The Defensive GOAT**

Several players could earn this spot, but we give it to Taylor, the great New York Giants linebacker. His speed and tackling skill changed how defence was played in the 1980s.

**Deacon Jones** played defensive end for the LA Rams. He started using the word "sack" in the 1960s. He said a sack was where he wanted to put opposing passers.

**Reggie White** was called the "Minister of Defence". He was one of the NFL's best-ever sack masters. And he was a church minister when he wasn't on the field!

In today's NFL, Pittsburgh's T. J. Watt is a sacking star. Like his brother J. J., Watt has been an NFL Defensive Player of the Year. Dallas's **Micah Parsons** is the second player to have at least 13 sacks in each of his first three seasons.

Linebackers are American football's roughest, toughest players.

**Dick Butkus** even had a name that sounded tough! He knocked down runners for the Chicago Bears in the 1960s. Butkus didn't let blockers slow him down.

**Ray Nitschke** was another top 1960s linebacker. He anchored the Green Bay Packers team that won five NFL championships in the decade.

The best linebacker of the 2000s was **Ray Lewis** of the Baltimore Ravens. His fiery leadership put him above the rest.

### No Tackling Needed!
Lots of young people get a start in the game without tackling. Flag football is a speedy, fun game played at schools and parks. Instead of tackling, teams pull flags from a belt worn by the ballcarrier. This version of the game is much safer and can be played without protective gear.

When the ball is in the air, defensive backs get to work. They try to prevent receivers from making catches. If a defender catches a pass, it's an interception. The defender's team gets to keep the ball.

One of the best defensive backs ever was **Dick "Night Train" Lane**. In 1952, he made 14 interceptions. That's still the most anyone has ever made in a single season!

In the 1980s, speedy **Deion "Prime Time" Sanders** became a star on and off the field. He used his great speed to prevent hundreds of catches. His big personality brought him even more fame.

Today's top defensive backs follow in the footsteps of the greats. **Antoine Winfield** is a safety for the Tampa Bay Buccaneers. In 2023, he was the top-rated player in his position.

**Sauce Gardner** of the New York Jets quickly became one of the league's best with his speed and attacking ability.

# Clutch Kickers

*Just seconds are left in the game. The Ravens trail by two points, but they have one more play. Justin Tucker steps to the ball. He kicks it towards the goal posts. It goes through! That's three points for the Ravens.* **They win!**

Justin Tucker

The first kickers poked the ball with their toes. By the 1960s, kickers had switched to swinging their legs like football players.

Kickers like Tucker don't have to run, pass or tackle. They just kick the ball. Field goals are a key way for teams to score. After a touchdown, the kicker also tries a kick that's worth one extra point if it goes through the posts.

The whole team depends on the kicker. The best kickers are clutch in tough moments. **Adam Vinatieri** made a last-minute kick that won the Super Bowl for his Patriots team. And he did it twice, in two different Super Bowls!

Tucker holds the record for longest field goal at 66 yards.

43

# Championship Coaches

Expert coaches choose players, assign positions and design plays for teams to run. They need to be effective teachers and inspiring leaders.

The NFL has had many legendary coaches. **George Halas** ran the Chicago Bears for nearly 50 years, from 1920 to 1967. His teams won six NFL titles.

**Paul Brown** was an innovator in the 1950s. With the Cleveland Browns, he invented key plays. He created the facemask. And he put radios in QBs' helmets so they could communicate with coaches.

**Vince Lombardi** led the Packers to five titles in the 1960s.

**Bill Belichick** was the leader of the Patriots from 2000 to 2023. He worked with QB Tom Brady to win six Super Bowl championships.

Today's NFL players and teams are more popular than ever. And the sport is spreading around the world. NFL games have been played in five countries on three continents. Watch for a spiralling football coming your way!

### Women in the NFL
In 2015, Jen Welter joined the Arizona Cardinals staff as the first female coach. Women have held various jobs with NFL teams for many years. Amy Trask of the Raiders was the first to be a team chief executive officer. As of 2024, more than 200 women work at all levels of the NFL and its teams.

# Glossary

**Clutch**
Able to come through in a key moment

**Defence**
The players who work to stop the offence

**Durable**
Able to withstand damage or pressure

**Dynamic**
Energetic and exciting

**End zones**
Areas at the ends of an American football field where touchdowns are scored

**Interception**
A pass caught by the defence

**Line of scrimmage**
An imaginary line that marks the position of the ball at the start of each down

**Offence**
The players who control the ball and try to move it down the field

**Professional**
Paid to play sports

**Punter**
Player who kicks the ball to the other team when his team does not move the ball 10 yards

**Route**
The pattern of steps run by a receiver

**Sack**
When a quarterback is tackled behind the line of scrimmage

**Snap**
When the ball is handed or tossed to the quarterback from between the legs of the centre, a member of the offensive line

**Spiral**
A movement that is a rotation around a straight line

**Starter**
A player who begins the game for his or her team

**Strategy**
A plan to make something happen

**Swivelling**
Spinning and twisting in a confusing way

**Touchdown**
When the ball is caught or carried into the end zone, worth six points

# Index

Allen, Josh  21
Baugh, "Slingin'" Sammy  17
Belichick, Bill  45
Black players  23
Brady, Tom  15, 45
Brown, Jim  25
Brown, Paul  44
Butkus, Dick  38
coaches  44–45
college teams  6, 7, 9, 10–11
Cook, James  27
defenders  9, 34–41
Elway, John  19
field  8, 28
flag football  39
Gardner, Sauce  41
GOAT  15, 25, 31, 36
Graham, Otto  11, 17
Halas, George  44
Henry, Derrick  26
school American football  7
Hill, Tyreek  33
history  10–13, 16–17, 23, 42
Hutson, Don  30–31
Jackson, Lamar  20
Jefferson, Justin  28–29, 32
Jones, Deacon  37
Kelce, Travis  14
kickers  17, 42–43
Lamb, CeeDee  33
Lane, Dick "Night Train"  40
Largent, Steve  31
Lewis, Ray  39
linebackers  34, 35, 36, 38–39
Lombardi, Vince  45
Luckman, Sid  17
Mahomes, Patrick  14, 15, 20, 21
Manning, Peyton  19
McCaffrey, Christian  22, 26
Montana, Joe  19
Moss, Randy  31
Motley, Marion  23
National Football League (NFL) see also Super Bowl
Draft  20, 21
history  10–13, 23
number of players on a team  9
racism  23
records  19, 26, 31, 43
women in  45
Nitschke, Ray  39
offence  9
Parsons, Micah  37
passers  14–21
Payton, Walter  24
Purdy, Brock  21
quarterback (QB)  14–21, 29, 44
racism  23
receivers  8, 14, 28–33
Rice, Jerry  31
Roosevelt, Teddy  11
running back (RB)  23–27
rushing (running)  21, 22–27
sacks  34, 35, 36, 37
Sanders, Barry  25
Sanders, Deion "Prime Time"  41
Strode, Woody  23
Super Bowl
  coaches  45
  fans  6, 12
  players  7, 15, 19, 21, 33, 43
Swift, D'Andre  27
tackling  8, 9, 34, 35, 36, 37
Taylor, Lawrence  36
touchdown (TD)  8, 14, 15, 18, 21, 30–31, 43
Trask, Amy  45
Tucker, Justin  42–43
Unitas, Johnny  18
Vinatieri, Adam  43
Washington, Kenny  23
Watt, J. J.  37
Watt, T. J.  34, 37
Welter, Jen  45
White, Reggie  37
Williams, Kyren  27
Willis, Bill  23
Winfield, Antoine  41
women in American football  13, 45

47

# Quiz

Answer the questions to see what you have learned. Check your answers in the key below.

1. In what year did the league that's now the NFL begin?
2. Counting both teams together, how many players are on the field for an American football game?
3. Why was Marion Motley an NFL pioneer?
4. What is a sack?
5. What is flag football?

1. 1920  2. 22  3. He was among the first Black players  4. When a defender tackles a quarterback behind the line of scrimmage  5. A game in which players grab flags from opponents' belts instead of tackling them